THE GIANT BOOK OF
CLASSIC ROCK

MUSIC

Produced by
Alfred Music Publishing Co., Inc.
P.O. Box 10003
Van Nuys, CA 91410-0003
alfred.com

Printed in USA.

ISBN-10: 0-7390-9423-8

ISBN-13: 978-0-7390-9423-5

Piano keys: © Shutterstock / Ensuper, Brush stroke: © Shutterstock / foxie

Contents

50 WAYS TO LEAVE YOUR LOVER

Words and Music by
PAUL SIMON

50 Ways to Leave Your Lover - 4 - 1

AFRICA

Words and Music by
DAVID PAICH and JEFF PORCARO

Verse 1:

1. I hear the drums ech-o-ing to-night.___ She hears on-ly whis-

pers of some qui-et con-ver-sa - tion.

11

Africa - 8 - 4

Keyboard solo:

14

Play 4 times

I bless the rains down in Af - ri - ca.

I bless the rains down in Af - ri - ca.
(Add lead vocal ad libs.)

Gon - na take some time to do the things we nev - er

Outro:

had. Ooo, ooo.

Repeat and fade

ALL ALONG THE WATCHTOWER

Words and Music by
BOB DYLAN

* Original recording: all guitars tuned down a 1/2 step in Cm.

20

ALL MY LOVE

Words and Music by
JOHN PAUL JONES and ROBERT PLANT

1. Should I fall out of love, my fire in the light,___

the tides have caused the flame__ to dim.
one voice is clear a - bove__ the din.
his is the voice that lies___ with - in.

At last the arm__ is straight, the hand to the loom,__
Proud Ar - y - an,__ one word my will to sus - tain,__
Ours is the fire,__ all the warmth we can find,__

is this the end__ or just_____ be - gin?_____
for me the cloth once more to spin,____
he is the fea-ther in the wind,____ oh.__ oh.__ }

Chorus:

All of my love,__ all of my love,__ oh, all of my love___ to

All My Love - 8 - 6

28

All My Love - 8 - 7

29

All My Love - 8 - 8

BEHIND BLUE EYES

Words and Music by
PETER TOWNSHEND

*Harmonies sung 2nd time.

32

34

BIG YELLOW TAXI

Words and Music by
JONI MITCHELL

Bright beat ♩ = 120

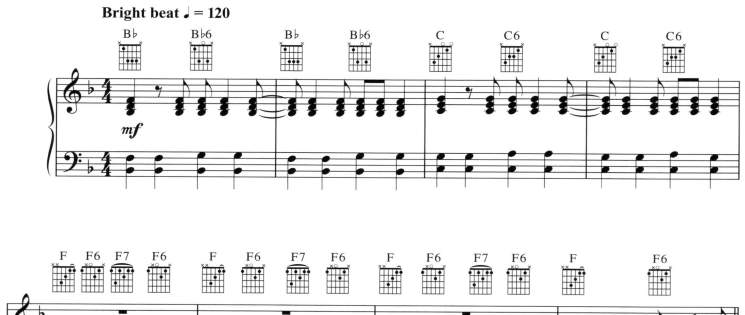

1. They

Verse:

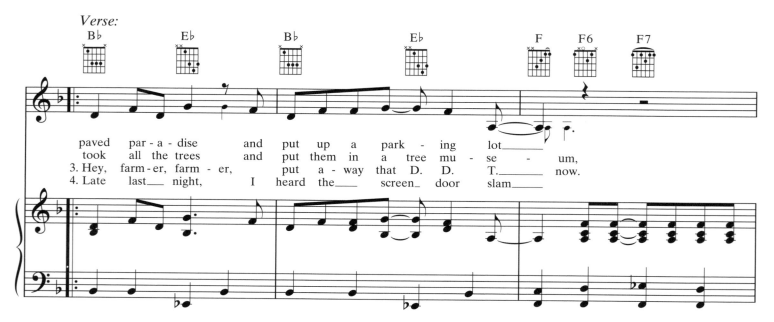

paved par-a-dise   and put up a park-ing lot_____
took all the trees   and put them in a tree mu - se - um,
3. Hey, farm-er, farm-er,   put a-way that D. D. T._____ now.
4. Late last___ night,   I heard the___ screen_ door slam____

Chorus:

38

(Woo,_____ bop___ bop bop__ bop.)   Woo,_____   bop__

_ bop bop__ bop.)   2. They   (Woo,_____ bop___ bop bop__ bop.)

Chorus:

Don't it al-ways seem___ to go   that you don't know what__ you've got_____ till it's gone?   They

Repeat ad lib. and fade

paved par-a-dise   and put up a park-ing lot._____

a tempo

They

BLINDED BY THE LIGHT

Words and Music by
BRUCE SPRINGSTEEN

Chorus:

ed   by   the   light,___   revved up_____ like a deuce,__ an-oth-er

run-ner in the night.   Blind - ed   by   the   light,___   revved up___

Blinded by the Light - 11 - 1

45

Blinded by the Light - 11 - 7

BORN TO RUN

Words and Music by
BRUCE SPRINGSTEEN

Born to Run - 10 - 1

56

Verse 3:

One, two three, four! 3. The

high-way's jammed_ with bro-ken he-roes on a last-chance pow-er drive.

Ev - 'ry-bod-y's out on the run___ to-night, but there's

no place left to hide.___ To-geth-er, Wen-dy, we can

Born to Run - 10 - 7

BRIDGE OVER TROUBLED WATER

Words and Music by
PAUL SIMON

Moderately slow ♩ = 84

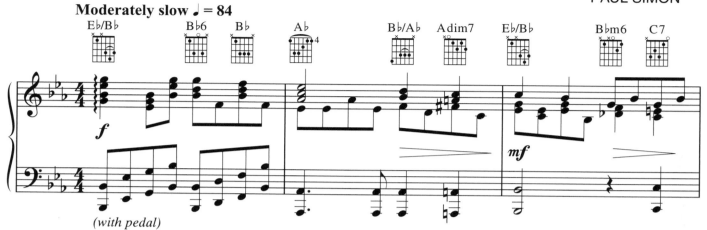

(with pedal)

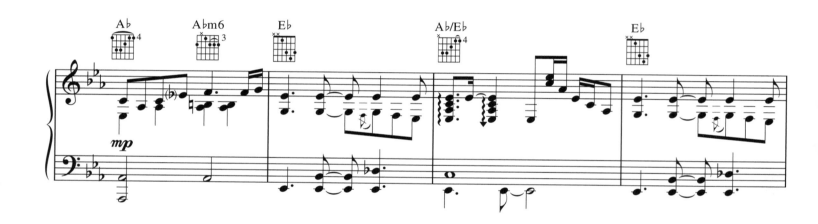

Verse 1:

1. When you're____ wea - ry,____ feel - in'____ small,

Bridge Over Troubled Water - 8 - 1

Verse 2:

BLOWIN' IN THE WIND

Words and Music by
BOB DYLAN

Verse 2:
Yes, and how many years can a mountain exist
Before it is washed to the sea?
Yes, and how many years can some people exist
Before they're allowed to be free?
Yes, and how many times can a man turn his head
And pretend that he just doesn't see?
(To Chorus:)

Verse 3:
Yes, and how many times must a man look up
Before he can see the sky?
Yes, and how many ears must one man have
Before he can hear people cry?
Yes, and how many deaths will it take till he knows
That too many people have died?
(To Chorus:)

CLOSER TO THE HEART

Words by
NEIL PEART and PETER TALBOT

Music by
GEDDY LEE and ALEX LIFESON

1. And the

Verse 2:
The blacksmith and the artist
Reflect it in their art.
They forge their creativity
Closer to the heart,
Closer to the heart.
(To Verse 3:)

Verse 3:
Philosophers and ploughmen,
Each must know his part
To sow a new mentality
Closer to the heart,
Closer to the heart.
(To Verse 4:)

Verse 4:
You can be the captain;
I will draw the chart,
Sailing into destiny
Closer to the heart,
Closer to the heart.

DANCING IN THE MOONLIGHT

Words and Music by
SHERMAN KELLY

Verse 1:

1. We get___ it on___ most ev-'ry night, and when that-a moon___ ___ gets big___ and bright,___ it's a su-per-nat-u-ral___ de-light,

ev - 'ry - bod - y was danc - in' in___ the moon - light. *(Inst. solo ad lib....*

...end solo)

𝄋 *Verses 2 & 4:*

2.(4.) Ev - 'ry - bod - y here___ is out - ta sight, but they don't___ bark and

they don't bite.__ They keep___ things__ loose, they keep___ things - a light.__

76

Chorus:

To Coda

Verse 3:

Ev - 'ry - bod - y was danc - in' in___ the moon - light.___ Danc-

in' in the moon - light; ev - 'ry - bod - y's feel - in' warm___ and bright.___

___ It's such___ a fine___ and nat - 'ral sight; ev - 'ry - bod - y's danc-

in' in___ the moon - light.___
3. We like___ our fun___ and we nev - er fight.

Dancing in the Moonlight - 6 - 3

DO YOU FEEL LIKE WE DO

Words and Music by
PETER FRAMPTON, JOHN SIOMOS,
RICK WILLIS and MICK GALLAGHER

Moderate rock ♩ = 112

Do You Feel Like We Do - 8 - 1

DON'T STOP BELIEVIN'

Words and Music by
JONATHAN CAIN, NEAL SCHON
and STEVE PERRY

Don't Stop Believin' - 4 - 1

90

FAITHFULLY

Words and Music by
JONATHAN CAIN

Slow rock ♩ = 66

1. High - way,

run   in - to the   mid - night   sun.

life   un - der the   big - top   world.

Faithfully - 4 - 2

94

Faithfully - 4 - 4

FOOL IN THE RAIN

Words and Music by
JOHN PAUL JONES,
JIMMY PAGE and ROBERT PLANT

Guitar continues simile

Oh ba - by.____

1. Well there's a

Verses 2 & 3:

prom-ised your love___ so com-plete-ly, and you said you would al – ways be
stand in the rain___ on the cor – ner, I'll watch the peo – ple go shuff – ling down-

true. You swore that you nev – er would leave_____ me, ba – by,___
town. An-oth-er ten min – utes, no long – er,

what ev-er hap-pened to you._____ And you thought it was on-ly in
and then I'm turn-ing a – round,___ 'round.__ And the clock on the wall's mov-ing

you,___ as you wished all your dreams_ would come true,_____ hey.
slow-er, oh, my heart, it sinks___ to the ground._____ And the

102

Fool in the Rain - 12 - 7

104

Fool in the Rain - 12 - 9

home.   I've got___ to get   home._____

106

Fool in the Rain - 12 - 11

Fool in the Rain - 12 - 12

FROM ME TO YOU

Words and Music by
JOHN LENNON and PAUL McCARTNEY

Moderate rock ♩ = 138

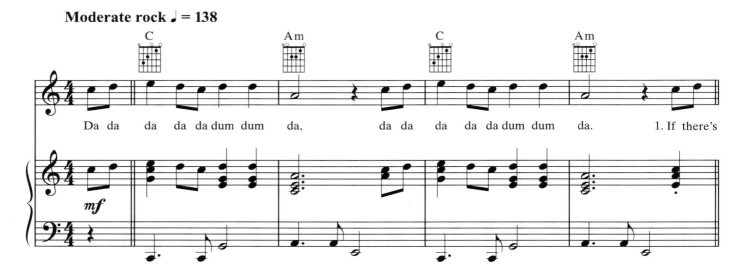

Da da da da da dum dum da, da da da da da dum dum da. 1. If there's

Verse 1:

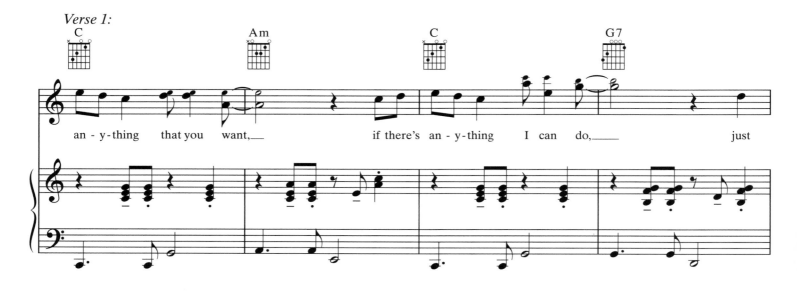

an-y-thing that you want,___ if there's an-y-thing I can do,___ just

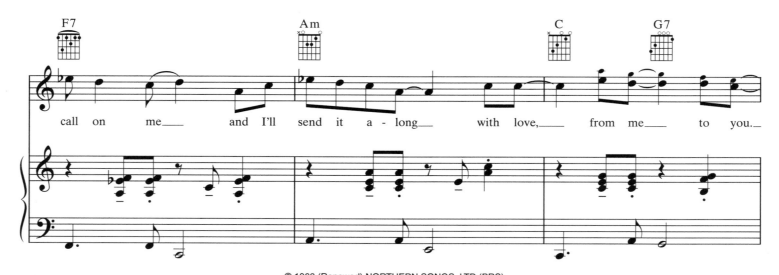

call on me___ and I'll send it a-long___ with love,___ from me___ to you.

*Vocal harmony 1st 4 measures second time only.

110

From Me to You - 4 - 3

GIVE UP THE FUNK
(TEAR THE ROOF OFF THE SUCKER)

Words and Music by
GEORGE CLINTON, BOOTSY COLLINS
and BERNARD WORRELL

Moderate funk ♩ = 108

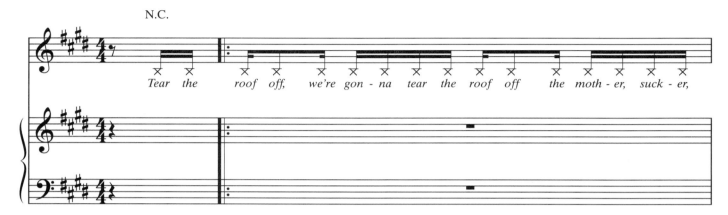

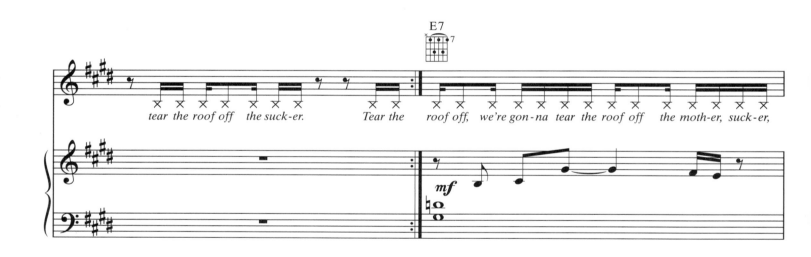

Give Up the Funk (Tear the Roof Off the Sucker) - 7 - 1

tear the roof off the suck-er. You've got a real type of thing go-ing

down, get-tin' down,_____ there's a whole___ lot of rhy-thm go-ing 'round._

You've got a real type of thing go-ing

down, get-tin' down,_____ there's a whole___ lot of rhy-thm go-ing 'round._

114

Ow,_____ we want the funk,

give up the funk. Ow,_____ we need the funk,

we got-ta have that funk. Ow,_____ we want the funk,

give up the funk. Ow,_____ we need the funk,

*Cue notes tacet 2nd time.

Give Up the Funk (Tear the Roof Off the Sucker) - 7 - 3

we got-ta have that funk.   La la la la la

doo   doo   doo doo   doo doo   doo,   ow!

La la la la la

doo   doo   doo doo   doo doo   doo,   ow!

Give Up the Funk (Tear the Roof Off the Sucker) - 7 - 4

116

THE GREAT GIG IN THE SKY

Words and Music by
RICK WRIGHT

The Great Gig in the Sky - 5 - 5

GOING UP THE COUNTRY

Words and Music by
ALAN WILSON

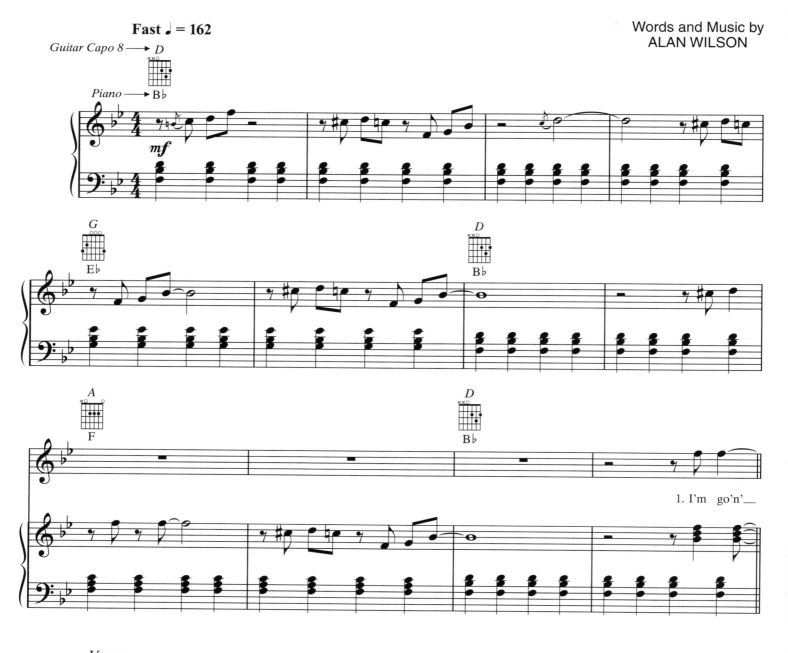

1. I'm go'n'___

Verse:

___ up the coun-try. Ba-by, don't you want___ to go?___

3.4. *See additional lyrics*

126

No use__ in you run-ning,_____ or scream-ing and

3. I'm gon-na leave__

Going Up the Country - 6 - 4

Verse 3:
I'm gonna leave the city,
Got to get away.
I'm gonna leave the city,
Got to get away.
All this fussin' and fightin';
Man, you know I sure can't stay.

Verse 4:
Now, baby, pack your leavin' trunk,
You know we've got to leave today.
Just exactly where we're goin' I cannot say,
But we might even leave the U.S.A.,
'Cause it's a brand-new game
And I want to play.
(To Tag:)

I LOVE L.A.

Words and Music by
RANDY NEWMAN

Hate New York Cit-y, it's cold__ and it's damp and all__ the peo-ple dress like__ __mon-keys. Let's leave Chi-ca-go to the__ es-ki-mos. That town's a lit-tle bit too rug-ged for you and me, you bad girl.

I Love L.A. - 8 - 1

132

134

I Love L.A. - 8 - 5

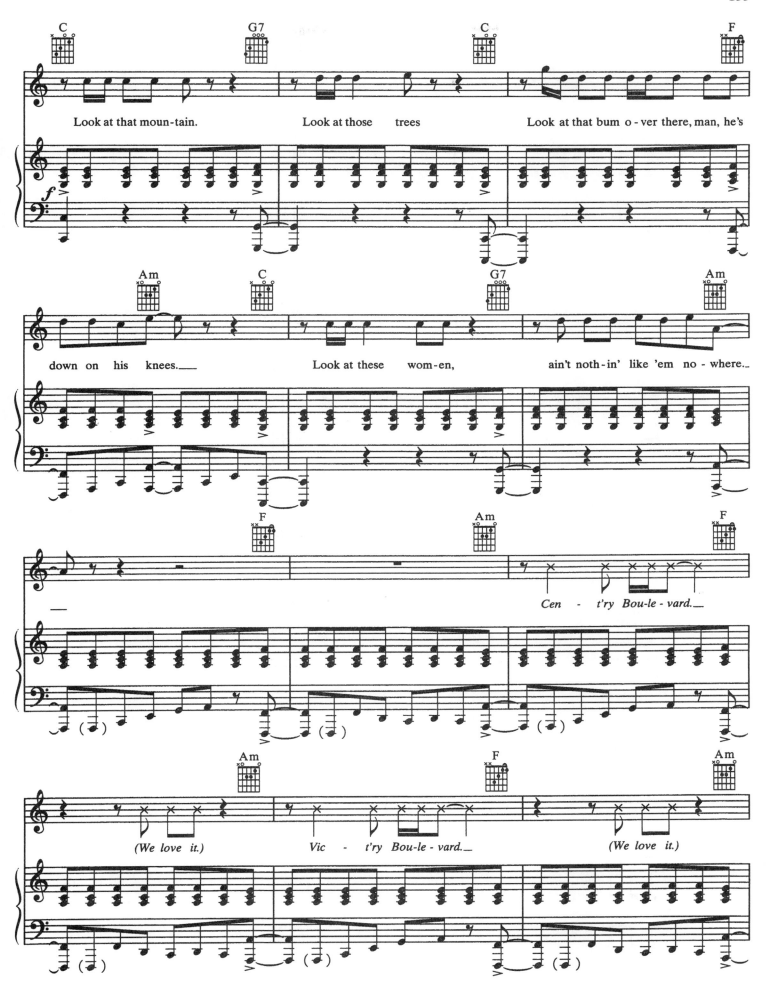

136

I Love L.A. - 8 - 7

I SAW HER STANDING THERE

Words and Music by
JOHN LENNON and PAUL McCARTNEY

Verses 1 & 2:

sev-en-teen,___ and you know what I mean.
looked at me___ and I,___ I___ could see___

And the way she looked was way be-yond com-pare.
that be-fore too long I___ fell in love___ with her.___

Guitar solo:

LIKE A ROLLING STONE

Words and Music by
BOB DYLAN

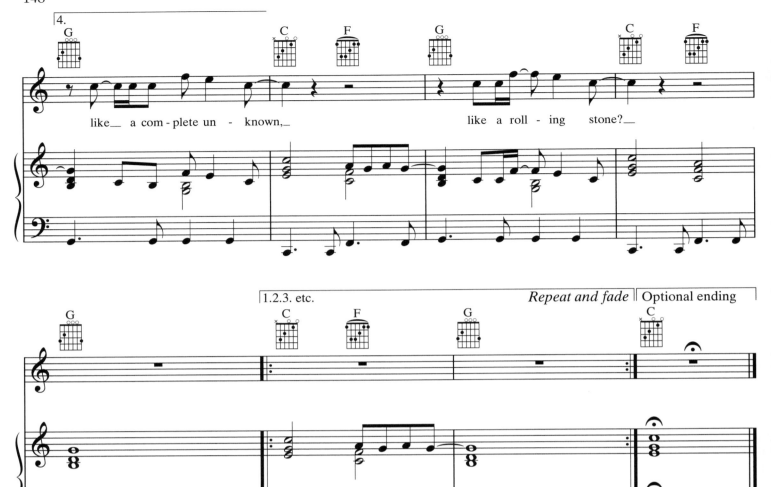

Verse 4:
Princess on the steeple and all the pretty people,
They're all drinkin', thinkin' that they got it made.
Exchanging all precious gifts,
But you better take your diamond ring,
You'd better pawn it, babe.
You used to be so amused
At Napoleon in rags and the language that he used.
Go to him now, he calls you, you can't refuse.
When you got nothin', you got nothin' to lose.
You're invisible now, you got no secrets to conceal.
(To Chorus:)

THE LOAD OUT

Words and Music by
JACKSON BROWNE
and BRYAN GAROFALO

Now, the

151

The Load Out - 11 - 3

153

The Load Out - 11 - 5

154

LIVE AND LET DIE

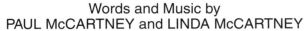

Words and Music by
PAUL McCARTNEY and LINDA McCARTNEY

Live and Let Die - 4 - 1

give the oth - er fel - low hell!

D.C. al Coda

Coda

LOVE REIGN O'ER ME

Words and Music by
PETER TOWNSHEND

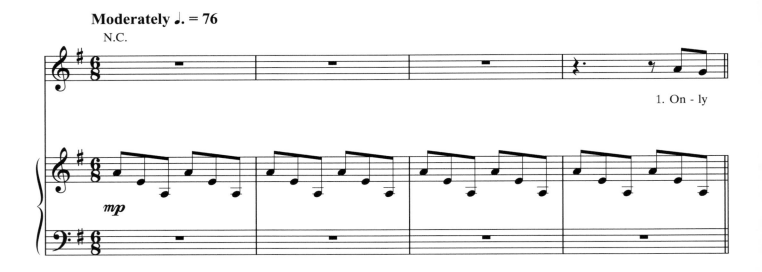

Verse 1: (Sing 1st time only)

Verse 2: (Sing 2nd time only)

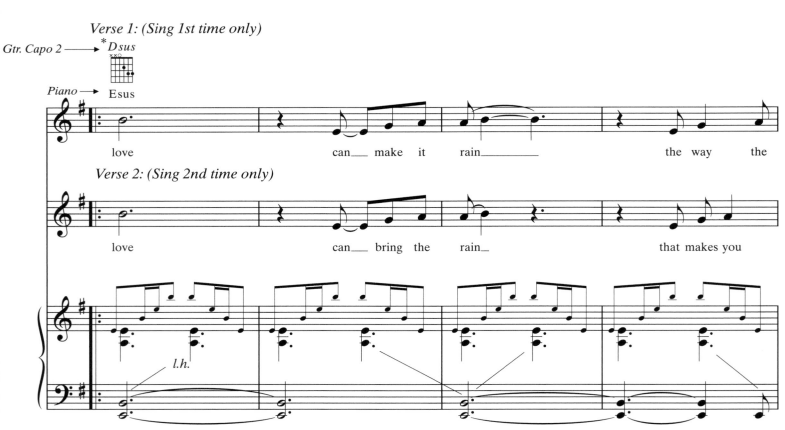

* Original recording down 1/2 step in E♭ minor - Guitar capo 1.

Love Reign o'er Me - 8 - 1

Chorus:

168

Love Reign o'er Me - 8 - 5

Oh God, I need a drink of cool,_____ cool__ rain._____

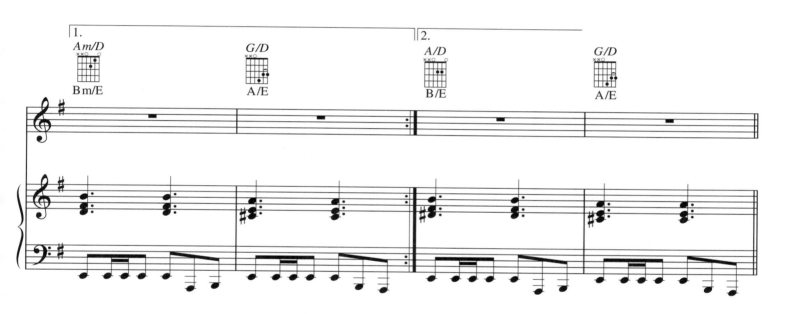

Guitar solo:

(Instrumental solo ad lib...

170

Love Reign o'er Me - 8 - 7

171

Love Reign o'er Me - 8 - 8

MONEY

Words and Music by
ROGER WATERS

174

sax. solo ad lib.

Money - 5 - 3

NIGHTS IN WHITE SATIN

Words and Music by
JUSTIN HAYWARD

Nights in White Satin - 3 - 1

178

Nights in White Satin - 3 - 2

Nights in White Satin - 3 - 3

PARANOID

Words and Music by
FRANK IOMMI, JOHN OSBOURNE,
WILLIAM WARD and TERENCE BUTLER

Fin-ished with__ my wom - an 'cause__ she could-n't help__ me with my mind.
I need some - one to_____ show me__ the things in life__ that I can't find.

Peo - ple think__ I'm in - sane be - cause I can't see__ the things__ that make__ true

Paranoid - 5 - 1

182

To Coda

satisfy.
I will cry.
Think I'll lose my mind if I don't find
Happiness I cannot feel and love

something to pacify.
to me is so unreal.

Can you help me
occupy my brain?

Oh, yeah.

Paranoid - 5 - 3

And so as___ you hear___ these words_ tell - ing___ you now___ of___

184

Paranoid - 5 - 5

PINBALL WIZARD

Words and Music by
PETER TOWNSHEND

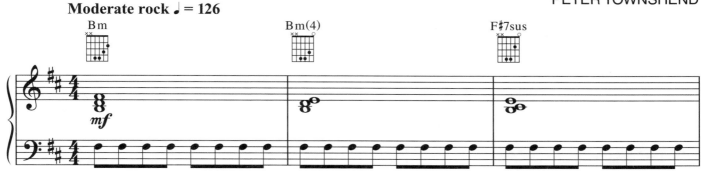

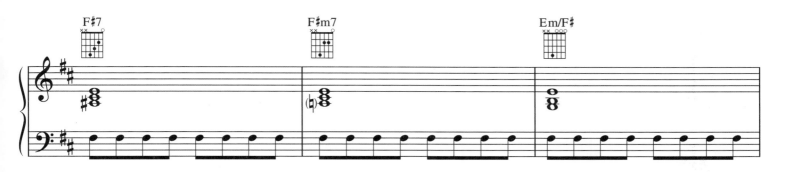

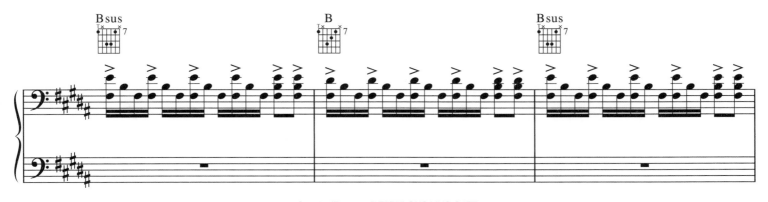

Verse 1:

1. Ev - er since I was a young boy, I played the sil - ver ball._ From So - ho down to Bright - on, I must have played 'em all._____ But I ain't seen noth - in' like_ him in

187

P-FUNK (WANTS TO GET FUNKED UP)

Words and Music by
GEORGE CLINTON, BOOTSY COLLINS
and JEROME BRAILEY

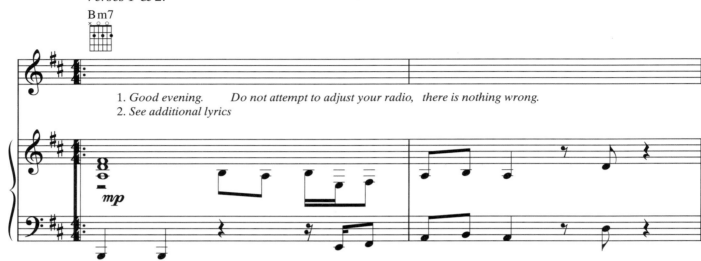

1. *Good evening.* *Do not attempt to adjust your radio, there is nothing wrong.*
2. *See additional lyrics*

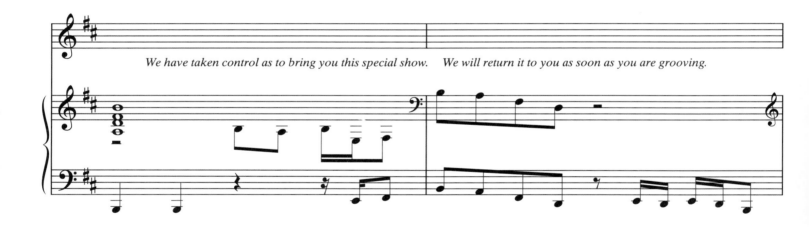

We have taken control as to bring you this special show. *We will return it to you as soon as you are grooving.*

Welcome to station W-E-F-U-N-K, *better known as We-Funk,*

P-Funk (Wants to Get Funked Up) - 10 - 1

or deeper still, the Mothership Connection.   *Home of the extraterrestrial brothers,*

dealers of funky music. P-Funk,   *uncut funk,*   *The Bomb.*

Coming to you directly from the Mothership,   *top of the Chocolate Milky Way,*

500,000 kilowatts of P-Funk power.   *So kick back, dig,*   *while we do it to you in your eardrums.*

194

Chorus:

1.

Make my funk the P - funk, I wants to get____ funked up._____

2.

wants to get____ funked up._____ Make my funk the P - funk, I

want my funk_ un - cut._____ Make my funk the P - funk, I

wants to get____ funked up._____ I want the bomb,_____ I want the P - funk, don't

Verse 3:

P-Funk (Wants to Get Funked Up) - 10 - 5

Y'all should dig my sun-rooftop.

Well, allright. Hey, I was diggin' on y'alls funk for awhile.   Sounds like it got a three on it though, to me.

Then I was down south and I heard some funk with some main ingredients,

like Doobie Brothers, Blue Magic, David Bowie.   It was cool,

198

Make my funk the P - funk be - fore I___ take it home.___

Solos:

Repeat ad lib. as desired | *Last time*

Chorus:

Make my funk the P - funk, I want my funk_ un - cut.___

mf

Repeat ad lib. and fade

Verse 2:
W-E-F-U-N-K, y'all.
Now this is what I want you all to do:
If you got faults, defects, or shortcomings,
You know, like arthritis, rheumatism, or migraines,
Whatever part of your body it is,
I want you to lay it on your radio, let the vibes flow through.
Funk not only moves, it can re-move, dig?
The desired effect is what you get
When you improve your Interplanetary Funksmanship.
Sir Lollipop Man! Chocolate-coated, freaky, and habit forming.
Doin' it to you in 3-D,
So groovy that I dig me.
Once upon a time called Now!
Somebody say, "Is there funk after death?"
I say, "Is Seven Up?"
Yeah, P-Funk!

RIVER

Words and Music by
JONI MITCHELL

⊕ *Coda*

way_____ on._____

Verse 2:
He tried hard to help me.
You know he put me at ease.
And he loved me so naughty,
Made me weak in the knees.
Oh, I wish I had a river
I could skate away on.
I'm so hard to handle;
I'm selfish and I'm sad.
Now that I've gone and lost the best baby
That I ever had.
Oh, I wish I had a river
I could skate away on.
I wish I had a river so long
I would teach my feet to fly.
Oh, I wish I had a river
I could skate away on.
I made my baby say good-bye.

SATURDAY IN THE PARK

Words and Music by
ROBERT LAMM

Saturday in the Park - 7 - 1

208

Verse 1:

1. Sat - ur - day___ in the park,___ I think it was the Fourth of Ju - ly.___

Sat - ur - day___ in the park,___ I think it was the Fourth of Ju - ly.___

Peo - ple danc - ing, peo - ple laugh - ing, a man sell - ing ice cream,___

(No octaves)

sing - ing I - tal - ian songs.___ (Ei-cay va - re, ei - se nar - de.) Can___

210

Saturday in the Park - 7 - 5

212

Verse 3:

3. Fun - ny days___ in the park;_ ev - 'ry day's the Fourth of Ju - ly.___

Fun - ny days___ in the park;_ ev - 'ry day's the Fourth of Ju - ly.___

Peo - ple reach - ing,___ peo - ple touch - ing, a real cel - e - bra - tion___

(Horns)

(No octaves)

SHE LOVES YOU

Words and Music by
JOHN LENNON and PAUL McCARTNEY

Moderately fast rock ♩ = 152

Chorus:

She loves you, yeah, yeah, yeah. She loves you, yeah, yeah, yeah. She

loves you, yeah, yeah, yeah, yeah. 1. You

Verse:

think you've lost your love, well, I saw her yes-ter-
said you lost hurt her so, she al-most lost her
know it's up to you, I think it's on-ly

She Loves You - 4 - 1

2. She ___ **Ooh,** ___ **she**

Chorus:

loves you, yeah, yeah, yeah. ___ **She loves you, yeah,**

yeah, yeah. ___ **With a love like that, you know you should be glad.**

To Coda ⊕

D.S. 𝄋 *al Coda*

3. You

SHE'S A RAINBOW

Words and Music by
MICK JAGGER and KEITH RICHARDS

She's a Rainbow - 6 - 1

220

She's a Rainbow - 6 - 3

air. Oh, ev-'ry-where, she comes__ in col ors __

Ooh, wah wah la la.

2. Have you seen her all in

1. **2.** *D. S.* 𝄋 *al Coda*

Bassoon

Strings

Coda

Guitar

THE SOUND OF SILENCE

Words and Music by
PAUL SIMON

1. Hel-lo, dark-ness, my old friend,

I've come to talk with you a-gain. Be-cause a vi-sion soft-ly

creep-ing left its seeds while I was sleep-ing.

*Original recording in E♭m, capo at the 6th fret.

The Sound of Silence - 6 - 1

when my eyes were stabbed by the flash of a ne-on light___ that split the

night and touched the sound of si - lence.

Verse 3:

3. And in the na-ked light I saw ten thou-sand peo-ple, may-be more.

Peo-ple talk-ing with-out___ speak-ing,___ peo-ple hear-ing with-out___ lis-t'ning.___

The Sound of Silence - 6 - 6

ST. STEPHEN

Words by
ROBERT HUNTER

Music by
JERRY GARCIA and PHIL LESH

232

Moderately slow ♩ = 63
Bridge:

234

Verses 3 & 4:

E   D2   A   E

3. Did he doubt_ or did he try?_____ An-swers a-plen-ty in the by-and-by.
4. Saint_ Ste-phen will re-main;_____ all he's_ lost_ he_ shall re-gain.

D

N.C.

1.

Talk a-bout your plen-ty, talk_ a-bout your ills; one man gath-ers what an-oth-er man_ spills.
Sea - shore_ washed by the suds_ and the foam, been

a tempo

STAIRWAY TO HEAVEN

Words and Music by
JIMMY PAGE and ROBERT PLANT

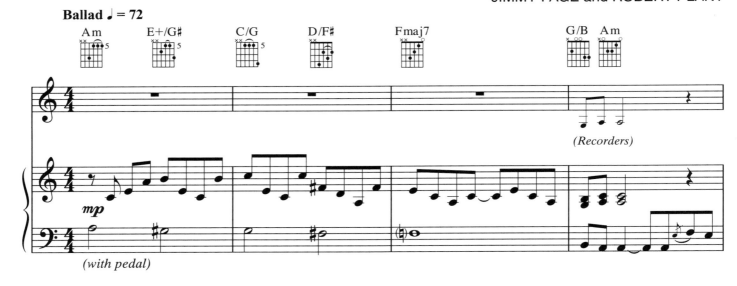

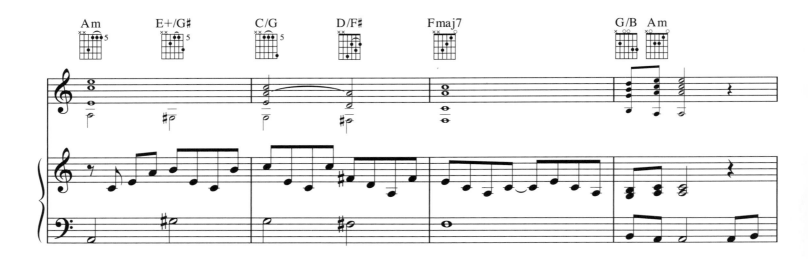

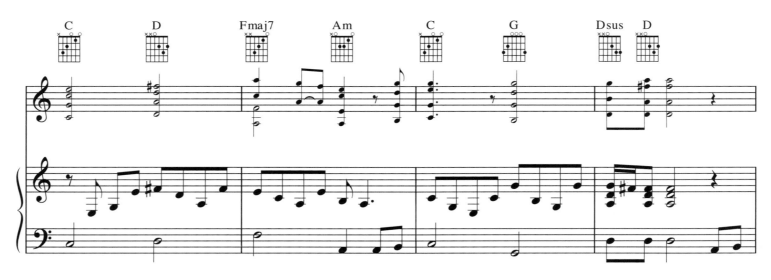

Stairway to Heaven - 12 - 1

Verse 1:

244

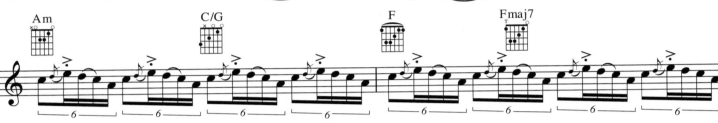

SPACE ODDITY

Words and Music by
DAVID BOWIE

Moderately slow ♩ = 72

Ground con-trol___ to Ma - jor Tom.___

Verse:

Space Oddity - 7 - 1

TOM SAWYER

Words by
PYE DUBOIS and NEIL PEART

Music by
GEDDY LEE and ALEX LIFESON

Moderate rock ♩ = 84

A mod-ern day war-ri-or,

mean, mean stride. To - day's Tom Saw-yer, mean,___ mean___ pride.

258

D.S. ℅ al Coda

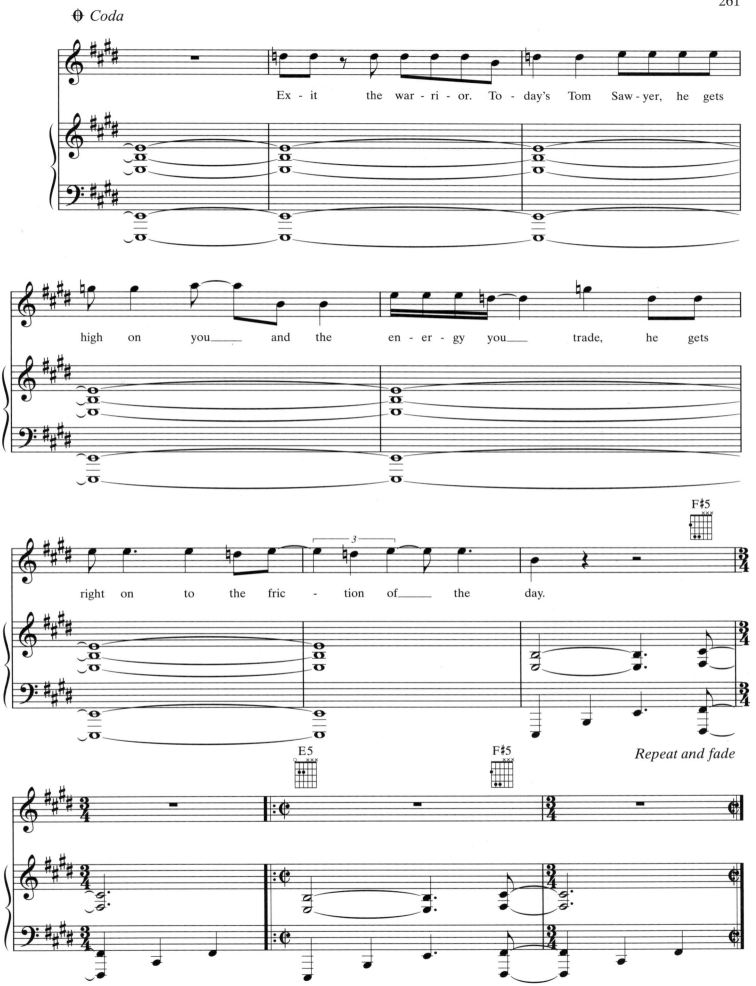

THUNDER ROAD

Words and Music by
BRUCE SPRINGSTEEN

Thunder Road - 10 - 1

full of los - ers. I'm pull-ing out of here to win.

Instrumental:

Tenor Sax.:

Repeat ad lib. and fade

UNCLE JOHN'S BAND

Words by
ROBERT HUNTER

Music by
JERRY GARCIA

Uncle John's Band - 7 - 1

274

276

A WHITER SHADE OF PALE

Words and Music by
KEITH REID and GARY BROOKER

1. We skipped the light fan-dan-go, _____ turned cart-wheels 'cross the
2. She said, "There is no rea-son, _____ and the truth is plain to

floor;_ I was feel-ing kind of sea-sick,
see."_ But I wan-dered through my play-ing cards

A Whiter Shade of Pale - 3 - 1

WOODSTOCK

Words and Music by
JONI MITCHELL

Moderately ♩ = 112

1. Well, I came

Woodstock - 8 - 1

Verse 1 (sing 1st time only):

Verse 3:

den.　　3. By the time_ we got_ to_ Wood - stock, we were half___ a mil - lion strong,_

and ev - 'ry - where_ was a song___ and a cel - e - bra -

tion.___ And I dreamed_ I saw__ the bomb-

er jet planes, rid - ing_____ shot - gun in the sky,_____ turn - ing

in - to but - ter - flies_____ a - bove our na - tion._____

Chorus 4:

We are star - dust, we are gold - en, we are caught_

(Star - dust,____ gold-

YOU CAN'T ALWAYS GET WHAT YOU WANT

Guitar in Open E tuning *(optional w/ Capo at 8th fret):*

⑥ = E ③ = G♯
⑤ = B ② = B
④ = E ① = E

Words and Music by
MICK JAGGER and KEITH RICHARDS

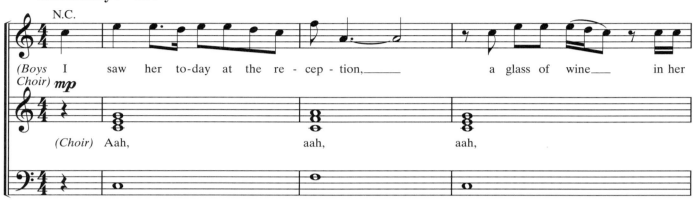

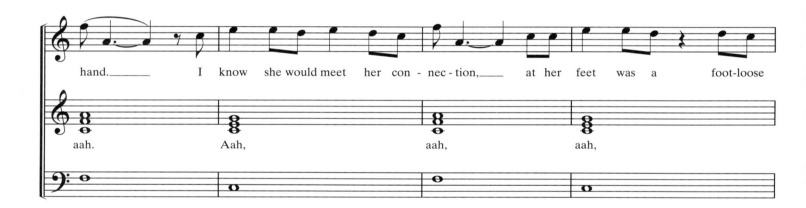

You Can't Always Get What You Want - 10 - 1

292

(Lead Vocal) 1. I

𝄋 *Verses 1 & 5:*

saw her to-day___ at the re-cep - tion,
5. *See additional lyrics*

a glass of wine_____ in her hand._____ I knew_

___ she was gon - na meet her con-nec - tion._____ At her

294

Verse 3:
I went down to the Chelsea drugstore
To get your prescription filled.
I was standin' in line with Mr. Jimmy.
A-man, did he look pretty ill.

Verse 4:
We decided that we would have a soda;
My favorite flavor, cherry red,
I sung my song to Mr. Jimmy.
Yeah, and he said one word to me, and that was "dead."
I said to him…
(To Chorus:)

Verse 5:
I saw her today at the reception.
In her glass was a bleeding man.
She was practiced at the art of deception.
Well, I could tell by her blood-stained hands.
Say it!
(To Chorus:)

WILD HORSES

Words and Music by
MICK JAGGER and KEITH RICHARDS

(Lead Gtr.)

(end Gtr.)

Verse:

1. Child - hood liv - ing_____
2. I watched you suf - fer_____
3. I know I've dreamed_ you_____

Wild Horses - 5 - 1

is eas - y to do.
a dull ach - ing pain.
a sin and a lie.

The things you want - ed,
Now you de - cid - ed
I have my free - dom,

I bought them for you.
to show me for the same.
but I don't have much time.

Grace - less la - dy,
No sweep - ing ex - its
Faith has been bro - ken,

we'll ride them some - day.

Solo:

(Lead Gtr.)

D.S. % al Coda

(end Gtr.)

Coda

we'll ride them___ some - day.